Sanjeev Kapoor's
KHAZANA

Eggs

Sanjeev Kapoor's
KHAZANA

Eggs

In association with Alyona Kapoor

Popular Prakashan
www.popularprakashan.com

Published by
POPULAR PRAKASHAN PVT. LTD.
301, Mahalaxmi Chambers
22, Bhulabhai Desai Road
Mumbai 400 026
for Khana Khazana Publications Pvt. Ltd.

First Published 2009
Third Reprint October 2015

(4225)
ISBN 978-81-7991-477-9

Design: FourPlus Advertising Pvt. Ltd.

PRINTED IN INDIA by
by Saurabh Printers (P) Ltd.
Plot No. 67 A-68, Ecotech, Ext. I
Kasna, Greater Noida-201306 (U.P)

DEDICATION

To the viewers of Khana Khazana and all my readers who inspire me to create new dishes and rediscover culinary treasures.

AUTHOR'S NOTE

An egg is one of the most nutritious foods known, as it contains all of the essential nutrients in a balanced proportion.

Once looked upon as a mere breakfast food to be fried, boiled, scrambled or whisked into an omelette, the egg appears today in various avtars on our tables. It is a versatile food, which can be eaten on its own, or added to curries. When whisked, it can form the basis for a velvety sauce or custard; the deep gold of the yolk adds colour and flavour and the frothy white adds lightness and air to a soufflé or a cake. Eggs also bind stuffings and fillings and glaze pastries and breads. Most of all, eggs add taste, nutrition and depth to even a simple recipe.

The jungle fowl was domesticated in India around 1400 BC and eating eggs was a natural progression right from those times. There is a reference to an egg-topped mutton dish in the 16th century work, Ain-e-Akbari and eggs are also mentioned in several Buddhist texts.

While they are considered to be a 'hot' food, eggs have always been known to increase one's strength and stamina and for that reason, wrestlers and athletes follow a diet enriched by eggs. Eggs symbolise birth, fertility and renewal. There are religious and cultural customs built around eggs, which have even been invested with cosmic significance. No wonder then that this white and gold delight has been, and continues to be, celebrated even today!

I have collected some of my favourite egg recipes for you in this book. Enjoy heart-warming Punjabi Anda Bhurji, Baida Roti - which is one of Mumbai's favourite street foods, silky Mushroom Quiche and sinful Chocolate Fudge Cake. There is a rich Egg Korma and the Parsi Wafer Per Eda.

Whisked, fried, poached or baked, ande da jawab nahin!

As always, each recipe serves four persons and has been tried and perfected just for you!

Here are some tips for storing eggs.

- Store them inside the refrigerator rather than in the door in an egg carton, broad side up.
- Eggs will keep at least for a week if stored in the refrigerator.
- To test whether an egg is fresh, drop it in a bowl full of water. If it lies at the bottom on its side, it is fresh. If it rises into a standing position it is less fresh and if it floats right to the top, it's time to throw it away!
- Eggs that are several days old hard-boil best. Once hard-boiled they can be stored in the refrigerator for three-four days in a covered container.

PACKED WITH GOODNESS

One large egg has:
Calories: 72 Kcal
Protein: 6.29 g
Carbohydrate: 0.39 g
Total Fat: 4.97 g
Saturated fat: 1.55 g } contained only in the yolk
Cholesterol: 212 mg
Vitamin A: 244 IU
Vitamin D: 18 IU

It also contains significant amounts of folate, choline, calcium, sodium, potassium, magnesium, iron and zinc - all essential nutrients.

Happy cooking!

ACKNOWLEDGEMENTS

Afsheen Panjwani
Anupa Das
Ashwini Patwardhan
Bharati Anand
Bhartendu Sharma
Harpal Singh Sokhi
Jayadeep Chaubal
Jayanthi Mahalingam
Jyotsna & Mayur Dvivedi
Mrs. Lata Lohana & Capt. K. K. Lohana
Namrata & Sanjiv Bahl
Neena Murdeshwar
Puja & Rajeev Kapoor
Rajeev Matta
Rita D'Souza
Sanjay Thorat
Saurabh Mishra
Shilpa Rane
Smeeta Bhatkal
Tripta Bhagattjee
Vinayak Gawande

CONTENTS

BOILED EGGS

Ingredients

Eggs at room temperature, or else the shell may crack while boiling.

Method

FOR SOFT-BOILED EGGS

Bring water to a boil in a pan. Reduce the heat. Gently lower an egg into the water and boil the egg for three minutes.

FOR BOILED EGGS

Bring water to a boil in a pan. Reduce the heat. Gently lower an egg into the water and let it boil for six minutes.

FOR HARD-BOILED EGGS

Bring water to a boil in a pan. Lower the heat. Gently lower an egg into the water and let it boil for nine minutes.

EGG WHITE OMELETTE

Ingredients

- 8 eggs
- 4 tablespoons oil
- 2 small onions, chopped
- 8-12 fresh button mushrooms, chopped
- 1 small green capsicum *(hari Shimla mirch),* chopped
- salt to taste
- white pepper powder to taste

Method

1 For each omelette, break two eggs at a time and separate the yolks from the whites.

2 Divide the onions, button mushrooms and green capsicum into four portions.

3 Heat one tablespoon of oil in a large shallow pan. Add one portion each of the chopped vegetables and sauté.

4 Place the egg whites in a bowl, add the salt and whisk till frothy.

5 Add to the pan and stir till the eggs are set. Sprinkle some white pepper powder. Drizzle a little oil along the sides, flip and cook the other side. Serve hot.

POACHED EGGS

Ingredients

4 eggs

2 tablespoons white vinegar *(sirka)*

salt to taste

white pepper powder to taste

Method

1 Heat two and a half cups of water in a pan. Place a metal ring in the centre of the pan. Add two tablespoons of vinegar. Break an egg into a bowl and slowly slide it into the water and cook on low heat.

2 As the white begins to coagulate, gently spoon it over the yolk.

3 Gently separate the egg from the ring with a knife and remove the ring. Carefully lift the egg out with a slotted spoon and dip in cold water. Once again, carefully lift it with a slotted spoon and place on a serving plate.

4 Sprinkle salt and white pepper powder and serve.

MICROWAVED OMELETTE

Ingredients

- 8 eggs
- 2 medium onions, finely chopped
- 4-6 green chillies, finely chopped
- a few sprigs of fresh coriander *(hara dhania)*, chopped
- 4 tablespoons milk
- salt to taste
- ¼ teaspoon white pepper powder
- 4 tablespoons butter

Method

1 Beat the eggs and stir in the chopped onions, chillies, coriander, milk, salt and white pepper powder. Divide the mixture into four equal portions.

2 For each omelette, place one tablespoon of butter in a flat microwave-safe dish and cook, uncovered, on HIGH (100%) for twenty seconds. Spread evenly and pour one part of the egg mixture into the dish, ensuring that it spreads evenly.

3 Cook, uncovered, on HIGH (100%) for three minutes. Leave to stand for one minute and serve.

STUFFED OMELETTE

Ingredients

8 eggs

salt to taste

black pepper *(kali mirch)* powder to taste

4 tablespoons oil

8 fresh button mushrooms, finely chopped

2 medium onions, finely chopped

2 medium tomatoes, finely chopped

2 medium green capsicums *(hari Shimla mirch)*, seeded and finely chopped

8 tablespoons grated cheese

Method

1 For each omelette, beat four eggs in a bowl with the salt and black pepper powder.

2 Heat two tablespoons of oil in a non-stick pan and sauté half the mushrooms, onions, tomatoes and capsicums for two to three minutes.

3 Add the beaten eggs and when they firm up a little, sprinkle with half the grated cheese. Fold in the edges to resemble a cone, then fold the narrow end over. Serve immediately.

TOMATO EGG-DROP SOUP

Ingredients

- 4 medium tomatoes, finely chopped
- 2 eggs
- 2 tablespoons cornflour
- 4 cups Vegetable Stock (see below)
- 2 tablespoons oil
- 2-3 garlic cloves, finely chopped
- 1 inch ginger (optional), finely chopped
- ½ medium onion, finely chopped
- 4 tablespoons tomato sauce
- salt to taste
- 1 teaspoon sugar
- ¼ teaspoon MSG (optional)
- ½ teaspoon white pepper powder
- 2 tablespoons vinegar *(sirka)*
- 3-4 fresh coriander sprigs *(hara dhania),* finely chopped

Method

1 Break the eggs into a bowl and whisk lightly. Mix the cornflour with half a cup of vegetable stock.

2 Heat the oil in a wok or pan; add the chopped garlic and ginger and stir-fry for a few seconds. Add the chopped onion and continue to cook for one minute longer. Add the tomato sauce and chopped tomatoes and cook over a high heat for about two to three minutes.

3 Stir in the remaining vegetable stock and bring to a boil. Add salt to taste, sugar, MSG and white pepper powder. Stir in the cornflour mixture and cook for one minute, or until the soup thickens, stirring continuously. Add the vinegar.

4 Pour the whisked eggs in a steady stream, stirring gently to form threads. The egg will coagulate and float to the top.

5 Serve hot, garnished with chopped coriander.

VEGETABLE STOCK

Peel, wash and chop 1 onion, ½ medium carrot, one 2-3 inch celery stalk and 2-3 garlic cloves. Place in a pan with 1 bay leaf, 5-6 peppercorns, 2-3 cloves and five cups of water and bring to a boil. Lower the heat and simmer for fifteen minutes and strain. Cool and store in the refrigerator till further use.

BABY CORN AND EGG FLOWER SOUP

Ingredients

- 4-5 baby corn cobs
- 1 spring onion
- 2-3 garlic cloves
- 2 tablespoons cornstarch
- 1 egg
- 1 tablespoon oil
- 4½ cups Vegetable Stock (page 22)
- 2 tablespoons sweetcorn kernels *(makai ke dane)*
- ¼ tsp white pepper powder
- ¼ teaspoon MSG
- salt to taste

Method

1 Wash and thinly slice the baby corn cobs. Wash, trim and chop the spring onion and reserve some spring onion greens for garnishing. Peel and crush the garlic.

2 Blend the cornstarch in half a cup of water.

3 Separate the egg white and keep the yolk aside for another recipe. Beat the egg white lightly and keep aside.

4 Heat the oil in a wok, add the crushed garlic and stir-fry briefly. Add the chopped spring onion and cook for two to three minutes on a high heat. Add the thinly sliced

baby corn and continue to cook for a minute more.

5 Add the vegetable stock along with the sweetcorn kernels and bring to a boil. Add the white pepper powder, MSG and salt to taste.

6 Stir the blended cornstarch into the soup, stirring continuously. Bring it to a boil and cook for a minute.

7 Reduce the heat and pour a spoonful of the beaten egg white into the simmering soup. Let it come up to the surface in the form of a white flower. Repeat till all the beaten egg white is used.

8 Garnish with the reserved spring onion greens and serve piping hot.

CHEF'S TIP

Use frozen or canned sweetcorn kernels for best results. If you are using fresh sweetcorn kernels, then pre-cook them till they are soft.

CHEF'S SALAD

Ingredients

- 1 medium head of iceberg lettuce
- 3 hard-boiled eggs
- 4 black olives, stoned and chopped
- 4 green olives, stoned and chopped
- 4 red radishes, chopped
- ½ cup grated cheese
- 1 garlic clove, chopped
- ½ cup French Dressing (page 95)
- 2 medium tomatoes, quartered

Method

1. Tear the lettuce leaves roughly into bite-size pieces and soak in chilled water. Drain.
2. Cut the boiled eggs lengthways into eight slices.
3. Place the lettuce in a bowl; add the olives, radishes, eggs, cheese and garlic.
4. Pour the French dressing over the salad and toss well.
5. Serve garnished with tomatoes.

SALADE NIÇOISE

Ingredients

1 medium head of iceberg lettuce

4 medium potatoes

15 French beans

4 medium tomatoes, quartered

4 hard-boiled eggs, quartered

½ cup French Dressing (page 95)

10 black olives, stoned

Method

1 Tear the lettuce into bite-size pieces and soak in chilled water.

2 Boil, peel and dice the potatoes. Cut the French beans into two-inch pieces and blanch in boiling water. Drain and cool.

3 Place the potatoes, French beans, tomatoes and eggs in a large bowl. Toss once to mix.

4 Pour the French dressing over and using two forks, carefully toss the vegetables till they are thoroughly coated with the dressing.

5 Arrange the chilled lettuce leaves decoratively on a large, shallow serving platter. Spoon the salad onto the lettuce leaves and garnish with black olives. Serve immediately.

BHURJI PAV

Ingredients

- 6 eggs, beaten
- 2-3 tablespoons ghee
- 2 medium onions, chopped
- 2 medium tomatoes, chopped
- salt to taste
- 1 teaspoon red chilli powder
- ¼ teaspoon turmeric powder *(haldi)*
- 4 green chillies, chopped
- 2 tablespoons chopped fresh coriander *(hara dhania)*

To serve

- 8 pav
- 2 tablespoons butter

Method

1 Heat the ghee in a *kadai*; add the onions and sauté over a medium heat for three to four minutes till light golden brown.

2 Add the tomatoes and salt and continue to cook over a low heat for another two minutes.

3 Add the chilli powder, turmeric powder and green chillies and cook,

covered, for one minute, or till the *ghee* separates.

4 Add the eggs and cook for two minutes over a medium heat without stirring. Continue to cook the eggs for another two minutes, stirring continuously.

5 Add the chopped coriander, cook for half a minute and transfer to a serving bowl.

6 Heat the butter in a thick-bottomed pan or a *tawa*. Split the *pav* horizontally in half and fry in the butter for half a minute, pressing down on the *pav* two or three times, till crisp and light brown.

7 Serve the *bhurji* accompanied by the *pav*.

BAIDA ROTI

Ingredients

Roti

- 1 cup refined flour *(maida)*
- salt to taste
- 1 tablespoon oil
- a pinch of baking powder
- 1 egg

Filling

- 8 eggs, beaten
- 1 tablespoon oil + for shallow-frying
- 1 medium onion, chopped fine
- 1 cup minced mutton *(keema)*
- 2 green chillies, chopped
- salt to taste
- ¼ teaspoon garam masala powder
- 1 tablespoon chopped fresh coriander *(hara dhania)*

Method

1 Mix together the refined flour, salt, oil, baking powder and egg. Add one-fourth cup of water and knead into a soft dough.

2 Divide the dough into four equal portions and shape into balls. Cover the dough with a damp cloth and set aside for a few minutes.

3 For the filling, heat one tablespoon of oil in a pan; add the onion and sauté till light brown. Add the minced mutton, green chillies and salt and cook over a medium heat till the mince is cooked and completely dry. Add the *garam masala* powder and chopped coriander and mix well.

4 Roll out each ball of dough into an eight-inch square *chapati*.

5 Heat a non-stick pan and place the *chapati* on it. Place some mince *masala* in the centre and pour two tablespoons of beaten egg over. Fold in the sides to make a square package.

6 Pour some more beaten egg over and drizzle oil around. Slowly turn the stuffed *roti* over and pour a little more beaten egg so that the *roti* is covered with egg on all sides.

7 Gently fry over a low heat till both sides are golden brown and crisp.

8 Serve hot with Green Chutney (page 93).

EGG HOPPERS

Ingredients

- 4 eggs
- 2 cups rice, soaked
- 1 cup grated coconut
- 1 cup cooked rice
- 3-4 slices of white bread, soaked
- salt to taste
- ½ teaspoon soda bicarbonate *(khane ka soda)*
- 1 teaspoon sugar
- sesame *(til)* oil for shallow-frying
- 1 teaspoon red chilli flakes

Method

1. Drain the soaked rice and grind to a smooth paste.
2. Grind the coconut, cooked rice and bread slices to a smooth paste.
3. Mix the two pastes and add enough water to make a batter of pouring consistency.
4. Leave the batter overnight to ferment.
5. Just before making the hoppers, add the salt, soda bicarbonate and sugar to the batter. Whisk well.

6 Heat an *appam* (hopper) *tava* and grease it lightly.

7 Pour a ladleful of the batter into the pan and swirl it around to thinly coat the sides of the pan with a thicker layer in the centre. Drizzle a little oil around the hopper. Cover and cook for two minutes.

8 Break an egg in the centre of the hopper, cover with a lid and cook till the egg is done and the edges of the hopper turn brown.

9 Sprinkle chilli flakes, ease the hopper onto a plate and serve immediately.

Note: Traditionally, a dash of palm toddy is added to the hopper or appam batter to ferment it. Toddy imparts a slight sourness and a delicate, lacey appearance to the appam. If you don't own a hopper pan, a small omelette pan can be used instead.

DEVILLED EGGS

Ingredients

6 hard-boiled eggs

3 teaspoons lemon juice

1 teaspoon honey *(shahad)*

salt to taste

1 teaspoon green chilli paste

1 tablespoon fresh chopped coriander *(hara dhania)*

1 tablespoon unsalted butter, softened

¼ cup Mayonnaise (page 94)

a few sprigs of fresh parsley

Method

1 Shell the eggs and cut them lengthways in half. Scoop the egg yolks out into a small bowl. Set the egg whites aside.

2 Add the lemon juice, honey, salt, green chilli paste, chopped coriander and butter to the yolks; mix well with a fork.

3 Stir in the mayonnaise and mix well.

4 Spoon the egg yolk mixture into a piping bag fitted with a star nozzle Pipe into the hollowed out egg whites and refrigerate for two hours.

5 Serve, garnished with sprigs of parsley.

EGGS BENEDICT

Ingredients

4 eggs

1 tablespoon vinegar *(sirka)*

salt to taste

2 bread rolls

2 tablespoons butter

4 fresh basil leaves *(tulsi ke patte)*

Hollandaise sauce

4 egg yolks

2 tablespoons lemon juice

½ cup butter, clarified (see below)

salt to taste

5-6 black peppercorns *(kali mirch)*, crushed

2 fresh basil leaves *(tulsi ke patte)*, roughly torn

Method

1 For the Hollandaise sauce, whisk the egg yolks in a pan. Add the lemon juice and two tablespoons of water and whisk again.

2 Boil some water in a larger pan. Place the pan with the yolks over the boiling water and cook, stirring continuously, till thick and smooth.

3 Remove the pan from the heat and add the clarified butter, drop-by-drop, stirring continuously, till about half the butter is used up. Add the remaining

butter, a little at a time, till all of it is used up.

4 Add the salt and the crushed peppercorns and mix. If the sauce becomes too thick, place the pan over hot water again and whisk. Add two basil leaves and mix. Keep the sauce warm.

5 To make the eggs, heat some water in a pan. When the water begins to boil, add the vinegar and salt. Break the eggs, one by one, into a small bowl and then gently slide each egg into the boiling water. Gently fold the egg white over the yolk and cook till the yolk sets.

6 Transfer the poached eggs with a perforated spoon onto a plate.

7 Slit each bread roll horizontally in half. Spread each half with butter. Place the halved rolls, buttered sides up on a plate. Place a poached egg on each half, topped with a basil leaf. Spoon some Hollandaise sauce over the eggs.

8 Grill the rolls in a preheated oven for two minutes. Serve hot.

Note: Eggs Benedict are traditionally served on English muffins.

CLARIFIED BUTTER

To clarify butter, simmer it on a very low heat for 10 to 15 minutes and then strain it through two layers of muslin (malmal), making sure that the milk solids do not pass through. Butter is clarified to remove the water and salt.

EGG NETS

Ingredients

- 6 eggs, chilled
- 2 tablespoons oil + for greasing
- 6 coriander roots
- a pinch of salt
- 8 garlic cloves
- 20 white peppercorns
- ½ cup peeled, deveined and minced shrimps
- 4 tablespoons fish sauce
- 6 tablespoons sugar
- 2 tablespoons finely chopped lemon grass
- 6 medium onions, sliced
- 2 fresh red chillies, cut into strips
- 6 tablespoons chopped fresh coriander *(hara dhania)*

Method

1 Whisk the chilled eggs lightly in a clean, dry glass or plastic container.

2 Heat a non-stick wok and grease it lightly. Dip your fingers into the egg mixture and wave them rapidly across the wok, so that the egg drizzles onto the wok. Move your hand backwards and forwards, and from side to side, to form a

net pattern. It will be necessary to dip your hand into the egg mixture once or twice to make enough strands.

3 Circle the edges of the net with more egg mixture to form a border.

4 Remove the net gently and place on absorbent paper. Repeat the process until the egg mixture has been used up. The nets can be made several hours in advance.

5 Pound the coriander roots, salt, garlic and white peppercorns to a paste with a mortar and pestle.

6 Heat two tablespoons of oil in a pan and fry the paste till fragrant and golden brown. Add the minced shrimps and season with fish sauce and sugar. Sauté for one minute and remove from heat. Cool completely and add the lemon grass, onions, red chillies and chopped coriander.

7 Lay each net out on a board; spread some shrimp filling on the lower third of the net and roll the net up, gathering the ends in to make a cigar-shaped roll.

8 Cut into slices with a sharp knife and serve.

CHEF'S TIP

Do not over-beat the eggs as this will incorporate too much air, which will cause the eggs to bubble slightly and toughen on cooking.

NAAN SANDWICH

Ingredients

- 4 *naan*
- 2 tablespoons oil + for shallow-frying
- 2 large onions, chopped
- 2 medium tomatoes, chopped
- salt to taste
- 2-3 green chillies, chopped
- 2 teaspoons red chilli powder
- ¼ teaspoon turmeric *(haldi)* powder
- 3 eggs
- 2 large boiled potatoes, grated or finely chopped
- 2 tablespoons chopped fresh coriander *(hara dhania)*

Method

1 Heat two tablespoons of oil in a non-stick pan; add the onions and sauté over a medium heat till light golden brown.

2 Add the tomatoes and salt and continue to cook for another two minutes.

3 Add the green chillies, chilli powder and turmeric powder. Stir and cook for two minutes, or till the oil separates.

4 Add the eggs and cook for one minute without stirring. When set, stir lightly with a wooden spatula and cook till done.

5 Add the potatoes and chopped coriander. Mix well and remove from heat.

6 To prepare each sandwich, split a *naan* in half to make two flat rounds. Place a generous portion of the potato and egg filling on one half, spread evenly and then place the other half of the *naan* on top and press lightly.

7 Heat a teaspoon of oil on a non-stick *tawa*; place the *naan* sandwich on the *tawa* and cook over a low heat for one minute. Carefully flip the *naan* over, drizzle some more oil around and cook for another minute.

8 Remove from the *tawa*, cut into quarters and serve with Green Chutney (page 93) and onion rings.

Note: The naan used in this recipe are not the same as the familiar tandoori naans. They are more like Indian pizza bread and can be bought from Muslim bakeries or in Muslim localities.

ANDA AUR METHI PAKORE

Ingredients

- 8 eggs
- 1 cup fresh fenugreek *(methi)*, finely chopped
- ½ bunch fresh coriander, finely chopped *(hara dhania)*
- 1 large onion, finely chopped
- 2 one-inch pieces ginger, finely chopped
- 4-5 green chillies, finely chopped
- 3 spring onions, finely chopped
- 3 tablespoons gram flour *(besan)*
- ¼ teaspoon carom seeds *(ajwain)*
- ½ teaspoon red chilli powder
- ½ teaspoon cumin *(jeera)* powder
- 1 teaspoon *chaat masala*
- ¼ teaspoon soda bicarbonate *(khane ka soda)*
- salt to taste
- oil for deep-frying
- tomato ketchup or Green Chutney (page 93), to serve

Method

1 Bring some water to a boil and cook the eggs for about ten to twelve minutes or until hard-boiled. Drain and immediately plunge the eggs into cold water. Peel and chop finely.

2 Mix together the chopped fenugreek leaves, fresh coriander, onion, ginger, green chillies and spring onions. Sprinkle the gram flour and mix well. Add the carom seeds, chilli powder, cumin powder, *chaat masala*, soda bicarbonate and salt.

3 Add the chopped boiled eggs, sprinkle a little water and mix well.

4 Heat the oil in a *kadai*; scoop up some of the egg mixture with a wet tablespoon and gently drop into the hot oil. Fry the *pakore* in small batches without overcrowding the *kadai*.

5 Cook for two minutes, turning the *pakore* occasionally so they brown evenly. Drain on absorbent paper and serve hot with tomato ketchup or green chutney.

AKOORI

Ingredients

- 6 eggs
- salt to taste
- 1/4 cup milk
- 1 1/2 tablespoons oil
- 1 1/2 tablespoons *ghee*
- 1 teaspoon cumin *(jeera)* seeds
- 1 inch ginger, chopped
- 2 medium onions, chopped
- 2 green chillies, chopped
- 1 large tomato, chopped
- 1/4 teaspoon turmeric *(haldi)* powder
- 1/2 teaspoon red chilli powder
- 2 tablespoons chopped fresh coriander *(hara dhania)*

Method

1 Break the eggs into a bowl. Add the salt and whisk. Add the milk and whisk again.

2 Heat the oil and *ghee* in a *kadai.* Add the cumin seeds, ginger and onions. Sauté for a few minutes.

3 Add the green chillies and continue to sauté till the onions are lightly

browned. Add the tomato and mix. Add the turmeric powder and chilli powder and continue to sauté.

4 Add the eggs and cook, stirring continuously, till the eggs are cooked but not too dry.

5 Stir in the chopped coriander. Serve hot with bread.

Note: Akoori is the Parsi version of scrambled eggs. Just as coconut is an indispensable ingredient in the food of coastal communities in India, Parsis swear by the eda or egg! It is an important part of wedding and funeral rituals. Other famous Parsi egg recipes are Wafer Per Eda (page 63) and Kera Per Eda (egg on ripe bananas)!

ANDA PARANTHA

Ingredients

- 10 eggs
- 2 cups wholewheat flour *(atta)*
- salt to taste
- 1 small onion, chopped
- 2 green chillies, chopped
- 2 tablespoons chopped fresh coriander *(hara dhania)*
- ¼ teaspoon white pepper powder
- oil for shallow-frying

Method

1 Sift the flour with salt into a bowl; add water and knead to a soft dough. Cover with a piece of muslin *(malmal)* and set aside.

2 Boil four eggs for ten to twelve minutes. When cool, peel and grate the boiled eggs. Lightly beat the remaining six eggs with a little salt and set aside.

3 In a bowl, combine the grated eggs, onion, green chillies, chopped coriander, white pepper powder and salt and mix well. Divide into eight portions.

4 Divide the dough into eight portions and shape into small *pedas*. Roll out each *peda* into a big round *chapati* and

place one portion of the egg mixture in the centre. Fold in the sides to make a square. Roll out into a thick square *parantha*.

5 Heat a non-stick pan and place the *parantha* on it. Cook for one minute and turn the *parantha* over. Pour some more beaten egg over and drizzle with oil. Carefully turn the *parantha* over and pour a little more of the beaten egg on it so that the *parantha* is covered with egg on all sides. Fry over a low heat till both sides are golden and crisp.

6 Serve hot.

CHEF'S TIP

Use a minimum amount of flour for dusting when rolling out the paranthas. If the paranthas are covered in flour, they will soak in more oil when they are being cooked.

STEAMED EGG KATORI

Ingredient

- 8 eggs
- salt to taste
- 1 teaspoon red chilli flakes
- 1 small onion, chopped
- 1 small green capsicum *(hari Shimla mirch)*, thinly sliced
- 4 tablespoons processed cheese, grated

Method

1 Take four microwave-safe bowls *(katoris)*. Break two eggs into each bowl. Sprinkle some salt, chilli flakes, onion, capsicum and grated cheese.

2 Sprinkle some more chilli flakes on top and place the bowls in the microwave and cook, uncovered, on MEDIUM (60%) for two minutes.

3 Serve hot.

CHEF'S TIP

You can also steam the eggs in stainless steel katoris in a steamer or a pressure cooker till set.

POACHED EGGS ON VEGETABLES

Ingredients

8	eggs
2	tablespoons white vinegar *(sirka)*
20	spinach *(palak)* leaves, chopped
16-20	fresh button mushrooms, chopped
2	medium onions, chopped
	salt to taste
1	loaf of unsliced bread
10-12	slices chicken salami, chopped

Method

1 Heat three-quarters of a cup of water in a pan. Add the spinach, mushrooms and onions. Add the salt and cook for three to four minutes or till most of the moisture has been absorbed. Divide into four equal portions.

2 For each portion, heat some water in another pan. Add half a tablespoon of vinegar. Place a ring in the centre. Break two eggs into a bowl and slowly slide them into the water and cook over a low heat.

3 Cut the bread into thick slices. Place a slice on a serving plate and place one portion of the vegetable mixture on it.

4 Gently separate the eggs from the ring with a knife and remove the ring carefully. Lift the eggs out with a slotted spoon and place over the vegetable mixture.

5 Place the chopped chicken salami on the eggs and serve immediately.

CHEF'S TIP

You can also poach one egg at a time without using a ring. Crack an egg into a small, thin-lipped mug or a small custard cup. Holding the mug or custard cup upright, lower the base into the water, and then, slowly and gently, twist your wrist to turn the egg out into the water. Don't hold the mug in the water for too long, or the egg will stick to the inside of the mug.

FRITTATA

Ingredients

- 100 grams spaghetti
- salt to taste
- 2 tablespoons olive oil
- 1 medium onion, peeled and sliced
- 1 medium green capsicum *(hari Shimla mirch)*, cut into 1-inch pieces
- 1 large tomato, cut into 1-inch pieces
- 1 egg
- ¼ cup low fat milk
- 3-4 black peppercorns *(kali mirch)*, freshly crushed
- 50 grams mozzarella cheese, thinly sliced

Method

1 Preheat the oven to 190°C/375°F/Gas Mark 5.

2 Cook the spaghetti in three cups of boiling salted water till *al dente* (cooked, but still firm to the bite). Drain, refresh in cold water and drain again. Stir in one tablespoon of oil to prevent the spaghetti from sticking together.

3 Heat one tablespoon of olive oil in a pan and cook the onion and green

capsicum for two to three minutes, or until very soft.

4 Add the spaghetti and the tomato and toss lightly to mix. Add salt and toss again.

5 Beat the egg with a fork in a large bowl. Add the milk, salt and crushed peppercorns and mix well.

6 Transfer the spaghetti to a baking dish. Pour the egg mixture over and arrange the cheese slices on top. Bake for twenty to twenty-five minutes.

7 Serve hot.

Note: A frittata is an Italian omelette and it can also have a filling of vegetables or meat. A frittata made with pasta is a Neapolitan favourite (Neapolitan refers to the city of Naples). It is usually pasta left over from a previous meal and contains tomato sauce.

EGG KORMA

Ingredients

- 8 eggs
- 1 inch ginger, chopped
- 5 green chillies, chopped
- 2 tablespoons grated coconut
- 1 tablespoon coriander *(dhania)* powder
- 3 cloves *(lavang)*
- 1 inch cinnamon *(dalchini)* stick
- 2 green cardamoms *(chhoti elaichi)*
- ½ teaspoon turmeric *(haldi)* powder
- ¼ cup milk
- salt to taste
- 3 tablespoons *ghee*
- 8 cashew nuts *(kaju)*, chopped
- 2 medium onions, chopped
- 2 teaspoons coconut milk
- 2 tablespoons chopped fresh coriander leaves *(hara dhania)*

Method

1 Grind together the ginger, green chillies, coconut, coriander powder, cloves, cinnamon, cardamoms and turmeric powder.

2 Break the eggs, separate the whites from the yolks and put into separate bowls. Beat the egg whites till stiff. Add the egg yolks, milk and salt and set aside for ten minutes. Beat the mixture again and place the bowl in a large vessel containing a little boiling water. Cook till the eggs are set. Cut into cubes.

3 Heat the *ghee* in a pan and fry the cashew nuts till golden brown. Drain and set aside.

4 To the same *ghee*, add the onions and sauté till light brown. Add the ground masala and sauté till the *ghee* separates.

5 Add half a cup of water and bring to a boil. Add the coconut milk and the egg cubes and cook gently till the korma thickens.

6 Garnish with chopped fresh coriander and serve hot with rice or *paranthe* and Green Chutney (page 93).

PUNJABI ANDA BHURJI

Ingredients

- 8 eggs
- 4 tablespoons oil
- 2 medium onions, roughly chopped
- ½ inch ginger, grated
- 3 green chillies, chopped
- 2 medium tomatoes, roughly chopped
- salt to taste
- 4 tablespoons chopped fresh coriander *(hara dhania)*

Method

1 Heat the oil in a pan; sauté the onions till light brown.

2 Add the ginger, green chillies and tomatoes and continue to sauté.

3 Break the eggs into a bowl, add the salt and whisk lightly. Pour into the pan and cook stirring continuously till the mixture is almost dry.

4 Lower the heat and sauté till the egg mixture is dry. Add the chopped fresh coriander and serve hot with *ajwain*-flavoured *paranthe* or bread.

WAFER PER EDA

Ingredients

- 100 grams potato wafers
- 4 eggs
- 1 tablespoon oil
- ½ teaspoon cumin *(jeera)* seeds
- 1 small onion, sliced
- 1 green chilli, chopped
- 1 medium tomato, chopped
- salt to taste
- 1 tablespoon chopped fresh coriander *(hara dhania)*

Method

1 Heat the oil in a pan; add the cumin seeds and onion and sauté till golden brown. Add the green chilli and tomato and sauté till soft.

2 Add the potato wafers, salt and two tablespoons of water; cover with a lid and cook for a minute or two. When the wafers are soft and the mixture is hot, spread the mixture evenly in the pan.

3 Break each egg separately on top of the wafer mixture so as to cover the entire mixture. Cover with a deep lid, pour some hot water on the lid and cook over a low heat until the eggs are set. Garnish with chopped coriander and serve immediately.

BAKED EGGS WITH CREAMY VEGETABLES

Ingredients

- 4 eggs
- 4 tablespoons butter
- 1 medium onion, chopped
- 5-6 fresh button mushrooms, thinly sliced
- 1 medium carrot, diced and blanched
- 1 medium potato, peeled, diced and blanched
- ½ cup shelled green peas, blanched
- ½ cup sweetcorn kernels *(makai ke dane)*
- salt to taste
- 4 tablespoons fresh cream
- ¼ cup milk
- ¼ cup grated processed cheese
- ½ cup breadcrumbs
- 2 tablespoons fresh parsley, finely chopped
- 1½ teaspoons red chilli flakes

Method

1 Heat the butter in a pan; add the onion and sauté for a minute. Add the

mushrooms and sauté till light brown. Add the carrot, potato, green peas and corn.

2 Add the salt, fresh cream, milk and cheese and cook for five minutes.

3 In a bowl, mix together the breadcrumbs, parsley and chilli flakes.

4 Preheat the oven to 200°C/400°F/Gas Mark 6.

5 Pour the vegetables into a baking dish and sprinkle three-fourths of the breadcrumb mixture over the vegetables.

6 Break the eggs, one at a time, onto the vegetables. Sprinkle the remaining breadcrumb mixture and bake for eight to ten minutes.

7 Serve hot.

MUSHROOM QUICHE

Ingredients

Crust

1 Basic Shortcrust Pastry (page 92)

Filling

225 grams fresh button mushrooms, thinly sliced

1 tablespoon olive oil

½ tablespoon butter

1 garlic clove, crushed

½ tablespoon lemon juice

salt to taste

black pepper powder *(kali mirch)* to taste

1 tablespoon fresh coriander *(hara dhania)*, finely chopped

2 eggs

¾ cup fresh cream

¼ cup freshly grated processed cheese

Method

1 Preheat the oven to 190°C/375°F/Gas Mark 5.

2 Roll out the dough till a quarter inch thick and transfer to a nine-inch tart pan. Trim the edge. Prick the base all over with a fork.

3 Heat the olive oil and butter in a pan over a medium heat and stir in the mushrooms, garlic and lemon juice. Add salt and pepper powder and cook until the mushrooms dry out. Increase the heat and cook until the mixture is dry.

4 Add the chopped coriander and adjust seasoning.

5 Whisk the eggs and cream together; add the mushrooms and mix. Sprinkle the cheese over the base and pour the mushroom filling over it.

6 Bake for about thirty-five minutes or until puffed and brown. Cut into wedges and serve warm.

Note: Pronounced 'kish' (to rhyme with 'wish'), a quiche is a French dish. Quiche Lorraine is the most well-known. Made with heavy cream, eggs, bacon and cheese, it was once cooked in a cast-iron pan.

NARGISI KOFTA

Ingredients

- 6 eggs
- 1 cup minced mutton *(keema)*
- 4 slices of bread
- 1 teaspoon ginger paste
- 1 teaspoon garlic paste
- 3 green chillies, chopped
- ¾ teaspoon red chilli powder
- ½ teaspoon coriander *(dhania)* powder
- ¼ teaspoon roasted cumin *(bhuna jeera)* powder
- 1 tablespoon chopped fresh coriander *(hara dhania)*
- 1 tablespoon chopped fresh mint *(pudina)*
- salt to taste
- oil for deep-frying

Method

1 Hard-boil four eggs; cool and peel. Beat the remaining two eggs in a bowl and set aside.

2 Grind the minced mutton, slices of bread, ginger and garlic pastes and green chillies till smooth.

3 Add the chilli powder, coriander powder, roasted cumin powder, chopped fresh coriander, fresh mint and salt and mix well. Divide the mixture into four equal portions.

4 Cover each egg with a portion of the mince till completely enclosed. Smooth the surface with moistened hands.

5 Heat the oil in a *kadai*. Dip each mince-covered egg in beaten egg and deep-fry till golden brown and crisp on the outside. Drain on absorbent paper.

6 Cut each *kofta* in half and serve hot with tomato sauce or tomato chilli sauce.

Note: This dish gets its name from Nargis or the narcissus flower, known for its dazzling white and yellow beauty. When the meatballs are cut they reveal the white and yellow (yolk) of a hard-boiled egg.

EGG MOILE

Ingredients

- 8 eggs
- 1 cup shelled green peas
- 1 large potato, cut into ½-inch cubes
- salt to taste
- 3 tablespoons oil
- 4 curry leaves
- 1 large onion, ground
- 1½ teaspoons ginger paste
- 1½ teaspoons garlic paste
- 1 teaspoon cumin *(jeera)* powder
- ½ teaspoon *garam masala* powder
- ½ teaspoon turmeric *(haldi)* powder
- 2 tablespoons chopped fresh coriander *(hara dhania)*
- 3 green chillies, chopped
- 2 medium tomatoes, blanched and chopped
- 1 cup coconut milk
- 2 teaspoons lemon juice
- ½ teaspoon sugar

Method

1. Put the eggs into boiling water and cook for nine minutes. Cool and peel. Make a small slit on one end of each egg.

2. Cook the peas and potato cubes separately in salted water till almost done.

3. Heat the oil in pan over a moderate heat. Add the curry leaves and onion paste and sauté till light brown. Add the ginger and garlic pastes, cumin powder, *garam masala* powder and turmeric powder and sauté till fragrant.

4. Add the coriander, green chillies and tomatoes. Continue sautéing for two minutes. Stir in the coconut milk, half a cup hot water, salt, lemon juice and sugar.

5. Add the peas and potato cubes. Cover the pan, lower the heat and simmer over a low heat for about ten minutes or till the spices are well-blended. Uncover the pan, add the eggs and continue to simmer for three more minutes.

6. Serve hot.

EGG BIRYANI

Ingredients

- 6 hard-boiled eggs, peeled and cut in half
- 1½ cups Basmati rice, soaked and drained
- 2 tablespoons oil
- 1 inch stick cinnamon *(dalchini)*
- 2 green cardamoms *(chhoti elaichi)*
- 3 cloves *(lavang)*
- 2 medium onions, sliced
- 1 teaspoon ginger paste
- 1 teaspoon garlic paste
- 2 medium tomatoes, chopped
- 2 tablespoons chopped fresh coriander *(hara dhania)*
- a few fresh mint leaves *(pudina)*, roughly torn
- 1 teaspoon red chilli powder
- ¼ teaspoon turmeric *(haldi)* powder
- ½ cup coconut milk
- salt to taste
- 1 teaspoon *ghee*

Method

1 Heat the oil in a deep pan. Add the cinnamon, cardamoms and cloves and sauté for one minute. Add the onions and sauté till soft. Add the ginger paste and garlic paste and sauté till fragrant.

2 Add the tomatoes and sauté for two minutes. Add the chopped coriander and mint and continue to sauté for two minutes longer.

3 Add the chilli powder, turmeric powder and sauté for a few seconds. Add the coconut milk, two and a half cups of water and salt.

4 When the water comes to a boil, add the rice and *ghee* and mix well. Cover and cook over a high heat for five minutes. Lower the heat and continue to cook for ten minutes, or till the rice is tender and all the moisture has been absorbed.

5 Transfer the biryani to a platter, garnish with boiled eggs and serve hot.

SESAME AND EGG FRIED RICE

Ingredients

- 1 tablespoon toasted sesame seeds *(til)*
- 3 eggs, lightly whisked
- 1 ½ cups Basmati rice, soaked
- salt to taste
- 4 tablespoons oil
- 2 spring onions, chopped
- 3-4 garlic cloves, chopped
- 1 tablespoon soy sauce
- ¼ teaspoon MSG (optional)
- ½ teaspoon white pepper powder
- ½ tablespoon vinegar *(sirka)*

Method

1 Bring five cups of water to a boil; add the salt and soaked rice, and cook over a high heat, stirring occasionally. Remove from heat when the rice is three-fourth done. Drain and spread on a plate to cool.

2 Heat the oil in a wok; add the spring onions and garlic and stir-fry for a few seconds. Add the eggs and cook for half a minute, stirring continuously.

3 Add the rice and salt and cook for one minute, stirring and tossing continuously. Stir in the soy sauce, MSG and white pepper powder.

4 Add the vinegar and mix well. Sprinkle toasted sesame seeds over the rice and serve hot.

EGG AND COCONUT PULAO

Ingredients

- 3 hard-boiled eggs, peeled and sliced
- 1 fresh coconut, grated
- 1½ cups Basmati rice, soaked
- ¼ cup oil
- 1 inch stick cinnamon *(dalchini)*
- 2 green cardamoms *(chhoti elaichi)*
- 2 cloves *(lavang)*
- ½ teaspoon turmeric *(haldi)* powder
- 3 green chillies, slit
- salt to taste

Method

1 Grind the coconut with one cup of warm water and squeeze to extract thick coconut milk. Extract two cups of thin coconut milk from the residue, by adding more water.

2 Heat the oil in a deep pan; add the cinnamon, cardamoms and cloves and sauté for half a minute. Add the rice and toss for half a minute.

3 Stir in the turmeric powder, green chillies, thin coconut milk and salt. Cook over a high heat for five minutes. Lower the heat, add the thick coconut milk and half a cup of water and cook till the rice is tender. Transfer to a serving dish and decorate with egg slices. Serve hot.

CRUNCHY MUFFINS

Ingredients

- 1 ½ cups refined flour *(maida)* + to line the tins
- 1 teaspoon baking powder
- a pinch of salt
- 1 cup cornflakes
- ½ cup + 1 tablespoon butter or margarine
- ½ orange
- ¾ cup brown sugar
- 1 egg
- 2-3 drops vanilla essence
- ¼ cup milk

Topping

- ⅓ cup brown sugar
- ¼ cup walnut *(akhrot)* halves, crushed
- ½ teaspoon cinnamon *(dalchini)* powder

Method

1 Preheat the oven to 180°C/350°F/Gas Mark 4. Sift the flour with baking powder and salt. Lightly crush the cornflakes with a rolling pin.

2 Grease eight muffin tins with one tablespoon of butter and dust them

with flour. Grate the rind of the orange. Cream the remaining butter, brown sugar and orange rind in a bowl with a wooden spoon till light and fluffy. Beat the egg lightly with the vanilla essence.

3 Add the milk and egg to the butter-sugar mixture and mix well. Add the flour mixture and stir the mixture clockwise. Mix in the cornflakes. Correct the consistency, if required, by adding more milk.

4 Divide the mixture equally between the muffin tins.

5 Combine the ingredients for the topping and sprinkle over the muffins.

6 Bake in the preheated oven for fifteen to twenty minutes or till a skewer or toothpick inserted into the muffins comes out clean.

7 Serve warm.

CHEF'S TIP

To dust the muffin tins with flour, fill the tins with flour to the top, remove all the flour and lightly bang the tins so that all the flour is removed except for a very fine layer.

COCONUT KISSES

Ingredients

- 1 ¼ cups desiccated coconut *(bhoora khopra)*
- 3 egg whites
- a pinch of salt
- 1 cup caster sugar
- 1 teaspoon vanilla essence

Method

1 Preheat the oven to 160°C/325°F/Gas Mark 3. Grease and flour a baking tray.

2 Beat the egg whites with salt until stiff. Add the sugar gradually, beating continuously. Fold in the vanilla essence and desiccated coconut.

3 Drop the batter in small mounds a little apart onto the baking tray. Bake for about forty to forty-five minutes. Remove from the oven and transfer to a wire rack to cool. Store in an airtight tin.

Makes 35 cookies.

BAKED CHEESECAKE

Ingredients

Biscuit Crust

1 cup crushed arrowroot biscuits

50 grams unsalted butter, melted

Filling

2 cups grated cottage cheese *(paneer)*

2/3 cup cream

1/2 cup caster sugar

3 eggs, separated

grated rind of one lemon

1/2 teaspoon almond essence

To decorate

200 grams mixed fresh fruit, peeled and chopped

1/2 cup almonds, chopped

fresh mint *(pudina)* sprigs

Method

1 Grease a ten-inch round springform cake tin.

2 For the biscuit crust, combine the biscuits and butter and press into the base of the tin. Chill in a refrigerator for twenty minutes.

3 Preheat the oven to 180°C/350°F/Gas Mark 4.

4 For the filling, beat together the cottage cheese, cream, caster sugar, egg yolks, lemon rind and almond essence in a large

bowl, until smooth and creamy. Whisk the egg whites until stiff and fold into the cheese mixture.

5 Pour the mixture over the biscuit base and bake for forty-five minutes, or until the cheesecake has risen and the centre has just set. Remove from the oven and leave in the tin until completely cooled.

6 Carefully remove the cheesecake from the tin and chill in a refrigerator for at least one hour. Just before serving, decorate with the mixed fruit, chopped almonds and mint sprigs.

Note: A springform tin has a removable base, commonly used for making cheesecakes, pies and tarts.

CRÈME CARAMEL

Ingredients

- 3/4 cup sugar
- 4 eggs
- 2½ cups milk
- a few drops of vanilla essence
- ¼ teaspoon nutmeg *(jaiphal)* powder

Method

1 To make the caramel, place a quarter cup of sugar and one tablespoon of water in a microwave-safe bowl and cook, uncovered, in the microwave oven on HIGH (100%) for one and a half to two minutes or till it caramelises. Remove and pour into an ovenproof mould. Leave to cool and set.

2 Pour the milk in a microwave-safe bowl and cook on HIGH (100%) for five minutes. Remove and cool a little (it should be warm).

3 Preheat the oven to 200°C/400°F/Gas Mark 6.

4 In a bowl, break the eggs, add the remaining sugar and whisk gently to blend well. Add the warm milk and vanilla essence and mix again stirring gently.

5 Strain the mixture and pour into the mould with the caramel. Sprinkle

nutmeg powder. Cover the mould with foil.

6 Cook in the preheated oven for forty-five minutes. To check if done, insert a skewer or knife into the dessert; it should come out clean. Remove from the oven and leave to stand for ten to fifteen minutes. Unmould on a serving plate. Serve hot or cold.

CHEF'S TIP

When making caramel, ensure that the bowl or pan in which you melt the sugar is very clean. Sugar tends to crystallise around specks of dirt when being melted and this will make the caramel uneven.

CHOCOLATE FUDGE CAKE

Ingredients

- 115 grams dark chocolate, chopped
- 1¼ cups refined flour *(maida)*
- 1¼ teaspoons baking powder
- 150 grams unsalted butter, softened
- 1 cup Demerara sugar
- 1 teaspoon vanilla essence
- 3 eggs, beaten
- 2/3 cup drained (hung) yogurt *(chakka)*
- chocolate curls, to decorate

Icing

- 115 grams dark chocolate, chopped
- 60 grams unsalted butter
- 1 cup powdered sugar
- 6 tablespoons drained (hung) yogurt *(chakka)*

Method

1 Preheat the oven to 190°C/375°F/Gas Mark 5. Grease an eight-inch round sandwich cake tin and line the base with greased butter paper.

2 Sift the flour and baking powder together and set aside.

3 Melt the chocolate in a heatproof bowl over a pan of simmering water. Alternatively, melt the chocolate in a bowl in a microwave oven on HIGH (100%) for one minute.

4 Cream the butter with the sugar till light and fluffy. Beat in the vanilla essence, then gradually add the beaten eggs, beating well after each addition. Stir in the melted chocolate and drained yogurt. Fold in the flour.

5 Pour the batter into the prepared cake tin and bake for twenty to twenty-five minutes, or until firm to the touch. Turn out onto a wire rack to cool. When completely cold, cut the cake in half horizontally.

6 To make the icing, melt the dark chocolate and unsalted butter as above. Stir in the powdered sugar and drained yogurt. Stir the mixture with a rubber spatula until smooth; beat until the icing begins to cool and thicken slightly. Use about a third of the mixture to sandwich the cooled cake halves.

7 Working quickly, spread the remaining icing over the top and decorate with chocolate curls.

CHEF'S TIP

If the icing begins to set too quickly, heat it gently to soften and beat in a little extra yogurt if necessary.

CRÈME BRÛLÉE

Ingredients

- 2½ cups fresh cream
- 4 egg yolks
- 1 whole egg
- 75 grams sugar
- a few drops of vanilla essence
- 6 tablespoons Demerara sugar

Method

1 Heat the cream in a pan till it reaches boiling point. Set aside to cool.

2 Preheat the oven to 180°C/350°F/Gas Mark 4.

3 Place the egg yolks and whole egg in a bowl; add sugar and mix well. Cook over a pan of hot water till the sugar dissolves, making sure that the eggs do not scramble.

4 Add the egg mixture to the cream and mix well. Stir in the vanilla essence. Strain the mixture.

5 Pour the strained mixture into six ramekin moulds. Pour some water into a baking tin. Place the moulds in the water bath and place the tray in the preheated oven. Bake for twenty to twenty-five minutes.

6 Remove from the oven. Take the moulds out of the water bath and leave

to cool to room temperature. Chill in the refrigerator.

7 Just before serving, sprinkle one tablespoon of the Demerara sugar over each portion of custard and brown with a chef's torch or under a grill.

8 Serve immediately.

Note: Crème brûlée literally means 'burnt cream'. To 'brûlée' means to caramelize the sugar topping with a small propane torch especially meant for kitchen use.

BASIC SHORTCRUST PASTRY

Ingredients

1 cup refined flour *(maida)*

60 grams butter, chilled and chopped

Method

1 Place the flour and butter in a food processor and process until the mixture resembles coarse breadcrumbs. If mixing by hand, rub the butter into the flour with your fingertips.

2 With the processor running, add drops of iced water until the dough comes together. If not using a processor, mix in the iced water with a knife or a wooden spoon. You can mix the dough by hand without handling the dough too much. You will need approximately two and a half tablespoons of water.

3 Press the dough into a ball, wrap in greaseproof paper or cling film and refrigerate for at least thirty minutes before rolling or shaping. Makes enough for one 9-inch pastry base.

Note: Shortcrust pastry can be stored in a refrigerator for two days, or in the freezer for upto three months

GREEN CHUTNEY

Ingredients

- 1 cup fresh coriander leaves, roughly chopped
- ½ cup fresh mint leaves, roughly chopped
- 2-3 green chillies, deseeded and chopped
- black salt to taste
- ¼ teaspoon sugar
- 1 teaspoon lemon juice

Method

1 In a blender, process chopped coriander and mint leaves with chopped green chillies. Make a smooth paste using a little water if required.

2 Add black salt and sugar.

3 Transfer to a bowl and stir in the lemon juice.

CHEF'S TIP

You can use crushed dried pomegranate seeds (anardana) or dried mango powder (amchur) instead of yogurt and lemon juice. In season unripe green mango is a good substitute. Add one cup of yogurt to two tablespoons of chutney for a completely different flavour.

MAYONNAISE

Ingredients

- 1 egg yolk
- salt to taste
- 1/4 teaspoon white pepper powder
- 1/4 teaspoon French mustard
- 1/4 teaspoon sugar
- 1 teaspoon vinegar *(sirka)*
- 1 cup oil
- 1 teaspoon lemon juice

Method

1 Place the egg yolk, salt, white pepper powder, mustard powder, sugar and vinegar in a clean bowl and mix thoroughly with a whisk. Alternatively, process the mixture in a blender.

2 Add oil, a little at a time, whisking or blending continuously, until all the oil is incorporated.

3 Finish the sauce by adding lemon juice; adjust seasoning.

4 Store in an airtight jar in the refrigerator.

FRENCH DRESSING

Mix together ½ cup olive oil, 1½ tablespoons vinegar *(sirka)*, 1 teaspoon mustard *(rai)* powder, ½ teaspoon freshly crushed black peppercorns *(kali mirch)* and salt to taste in a jar; close tightly and shake well to mix.

THOUSAND ISLAND DRESSING

Mix together ¾ cup Mayonnaise (page 94), 1 tablespoon tomato ketchup, 1 teaspoon Tabasco sauce, 3-4 chopped, stoned olives, 2-3 chopped pickled onions and 2 chopped pickled gherkins.